D1450746

DEAN B. ELLIS LIBRARY

WITHDRAWN
From the
Dean B. Ellis Library
Arkansas State University

THE MIRACLE
OF GREEK
SCULPTURE

THE MIRACLE OF GREEK SCULPTURE

with forty-seven drawings

by C. W. ANDERSON

Introduction by Jean L. Keith,
The Brooklyn Museum

E. P. Dutton & Co., Inc.
New York

To Madeleine

Copyright © 1970 by C. W. Anderson
All rights reserved. Printed in the U.S.A.
First Edition

No part of this publication may be reproduced or transmitted
in any form or by any means, electronic or mechanical, including
photocopy, recording, or any information storage and retrieval
system now known or to be invented, without permission in writing
from the publisher, except by a reviewer who wishes to quote brief
passages in connection with a review written for inclusion in a
magazine, newspaper or broadcast.

Published simultaneously in Canada by
Clarke, Irwin & Company Limited, Toronto and Vancouver

Library of Congress Catalog Card Number: 69-13358

*Lit Sci
733.3
An 23m*

Introduction

First and foremost, sculptures are three-dimensional objects and, in that respect, closer to the real thing being represented than a painting on a flat surface or a photograph. Second, and nearly as important, is the distinction between the two kinds of sculptural composition: *sculpture in the round* and *relief sculpture. Sculpture in the round* is truly three-dimensional, can be walked around, and has views from all sides. *Relief sculpture,* however, is intended to be seen from the front, and is often carved with the figures actually attached to a background (page 40).

Sculptors in all ages have used many materials, each one demanding special means in its handling. The Greek sculpture in this book exemplifies the three basic techniques of modeling, casting and carving. A very early method developed by man was modeling—forming an object or a figure of soft material such as clay or wax. The clay can be dried and then hardened by firing (baking in an oven). Either a clay or a wax object, if properly prepared, can be reproduced by casting in a more durable material like bronze or other metal. Carving, on the other hand, is an entirely different approach—it is cutting away from a block of material like ivory, wood or stone, as contrasted to the adding-on process of modeling. Stones have varying qualities of color, hardness, crystalline formation and grain that demand every skill of the artist in the selection of a block appropriate to his subject and of a sort that is within his craftmanship to cut and finish.

240996

Because sculpture is three-dimensional, it must be experienced: seen directly with our own eyes, which must be done primarily in museums now. But we can still enjoy it through photographs and drawings, as long as we remember that the figure, even the shallowest relief, has *depth* as well as height and width. Another consideration is the matter of scale: in looking at books on sculpture, it is easy to get the idea that the sculptures are really the size of the pictures, when actually, the pieces may be miniature, life-size or even colossal. To help us remember these variations in size, the height of the sculpture has been included here whenever possible.

Bear in mind that most of the pieces we see here were intended to be seen in special contexts, often out of doors. Some were designed to decorate buildings, primarily temples, thus have a religious as well as ornamental objective. Others have different religious connections—cult statues (representations of gods and goddesses) in temples and sanctuaries, votives (devotional offerings) dedicated by individuals or groups of people to a deity, memorial figures to dead persons (page 32).

Knowing something of the place where a statue was found can aid historians of art in reconstructing what its original purpose may have been. The most certain way is by means of excavation—digging up an ancient place under the supervision of a trained archaeologist who records every detail of the circumstances in which an object is found. But even this method is not infallible. Many ancient buildings and statues are still found by chance, as in the plowing of a field or the digging up of a street for subway or sewer. When a scholar is trying to identify the subject of a sculpture and when it was made, he can be most sure of his deductions when he is able to locate an excavated object that resembles it and has been reasonably dated by its "find circumstances." New excavations, both planned and haphazard, are continuously bringing to the surface new pieces that give us additional information about previously known sculpture. In fact, every "conclusion" concerning archaeology must be tentative, ready to be modified by new evidence, new clues to the mystery of how ancient peoples lived.

Some of the most famous of the works included here have fascinating histories that can be traced from antiquity. They have been in many places and in many hands before their present resting places, which are often so far removed from the place where they were made or found that the only way to gather together certain sculptures which were originally in one place is to put them in a book! The "Rampin Head" (page 30), for example, is in Paris, and the body of the rider and part of the horse are in Athens. The names that become attached to famous statues come from several sources. Sometimes they are named after a former owner, as in "Rampin Head," and "Farnese Herakles." In other cases the name describes the action of the statue, as in the "Diskobolos" or discus thrower. In still other cases, the name refers to the place where the statue was found, as in the "Nike of Samothrace."

That so much of Greek art existing today is in museums is a result of the respect and love for Greek sculpture that has been held by non-Greeks since ancient times. Among the early connoisseurs of Greek art were the Romans. In fact, it is partly due to their admiration for the Greek way of life and its artistic expression that we know as much as we do about it. There were cultivated, wealthy and powerful Romans such as the Emperor Hadrian, who preserved original sculptures and paintings and also had copies made directly from famous originals.

Much original Greek sculpture was made of bronze, especially when it was a statue in the round and life-size or over. We have few bronze originals because bronze was a useful material and easily reusable after being melted down. It also falls victim to destructive natural elements—corrosion resulting from dampness and salts in earth and air. Life-size copies of bronze statues were often made in marble in the second century B.C. and later. The original bronze sculpture was hollow and able literally to stand on its own two feet because of the strength of the material, but some added support had to be devised for the stone copies. A Roman copy of a Greek original standing statue almost always has a tree trunk (page 38), a dolphin, a pile of armor supporting one leg and often marble struts carved to anchor outstretched or free-hanging arms to thighs or shoulders (page 56). Some of the most renowned fifth century statues (for example, Pheidias' colossal gold and ivory statue of Athena Parthenos for her great temple on the Acropolis in Athens) are known only through copies often smaller in size and in different materials. Another aid to our knowledge of now-lost Greek sculpture are literary descriptions made by travelers and scholars in ancient times. Perhaps the most celebrated of these writers is Pausanias, who recorded buildings and artworks which he saw in the course of his extensive Mediterranean travels during the second century A.D.

It is also mostly through the accounts and critiques of ancient authors that we know the little we do about the sculptors themselves. In a very few cases, sculptors wrote down the principles by which they did their work. For example, Polykleitos wrote his canon (rules) of proportions for representing the male body, which is so admirably reflected in the Doryphoros (page 56). Occasionally a sculpture, or its base, was inscribed with the name of its maker.

One of the remarkable facts about Greek art is the steady development of its style without startling breaks or jumps. In the Geometric period, the human body was represented in its simplest abstract forms. Artists of the Classical period showed the figure in its real anatomic proportions idealized (made perfect). Later in the Hellenistic age, the many variations of form and movement of which the body is capable were used to achieve a great range of expression of feeling.

The names that we give various periods of Greek art are modern terms. While they may reflect some aspect of the artistic style, Greeks of the eighth century B.C. had no idea that they were living in the "Geometric period." More or less appropriate, these labels have become so widely accepted that we will continue to use them here, and to try to set the scene in which the sculptures were placed. The periods we will briefly summarize and their very approximate dates are:

Geometric period	900–650 B.C.	(ninth to mid-seventh centuries)
Archaic period	650–480 B.C.	(mid-seventh to early fifth centuries)
Classical period	480–400 B.C.	(fifth century)
Fourth century	400–323 B.C.	
Hellenistic period	323– 50 B.C.	(late fourth to mid-first centuries)

Among the earliest sculpture found in Greek lands are those of the Cycladic Islands, where sculptors were carving abstract figures of men and women in their fine local marble for burial and votive use in the third millennium (3000–2000 B.C.).

There are some sculptures remaining from the Minoans of Crete and the Mycenaeans of the Peloponnesos in the eighteenth to twelfth centuries B.C. These range from small ivory and pottery figures to life-size masks of the dead made of sheet gold to one monumental relief of lions set over the forbidding gate of the palace at Mycenae.

The Geometric period was richly productive of pottery decorated with the circles, stripes and other abstract designs, from which the period gets its name. The sculpture that we know from the same period is small in size, usually bronze, and reflects in the rendering of living creatures the same urge seen in pottery to reduce nature to its simplest and most straightforward forms (pages 20 and 22). Already by this time, the ninth century, Greeks had settled in Asia Minor (West Turkey) and had traveled as far east as North Syria. Their contact with Eastern peoples introduced new motifs, namely fantastic creatures such as sphinxes and real ones such as lions (page 24) as well as decorative plant elements which were to come to full flower in the Orientalizing ("easternizing") period that was a transition to the Archaic period (650–480 B.C.).

During the Archaic period, Greek colonies were established in the West, in Italy and Sicily, as well as in Egypt and on the coast of the Black Sea, and the Hellenic spirit and customs moved with the citizens and artisans. After the middle of the seventh century, monumental (life-size and larger) sculpture in stone became a tradition. The pose of the *kouroi* (statues of nude youths)—hands clenched to thighs, head and torso squarely front, legs front with the left foot moving forward—was possibly the result of Greek settlers' experience of sculpture in Egypt; differences in material and spirit produced quite a different effect, however. For over a century and a half, the *kouroi* developed and changed very little in size and style (pages 28 and 32). Finally, in the first quarter of the fifth century, dramatic new means of representing movement heralded the Classical age, the "Golden Age" of Greek civilization. The figures of young men were dedicated as memorials (page 32) to a dead youth or as followers of a god; few can safely be identified as gods themselves.

Relief sculpture of high quality existed in the Archaic period as decoration for architecture, particularly for temples, such as those on the Acropolis in Athens. (Nearly every Greek city had an acropolis, a "high-city" that was both citadel [fortress] and center of worship.) It was on such buildings that sculptors attempted more complicated compositions (arrangements) of several figures, in contrast to the conventional, straightforward pose-in-the-round of the *kouroi*. The stories told in sculptured reliefs usually referred to the deity or several gods to which the building was dedicated and contributed to its religious force; for example, on the Parthenon, the most holy temple on the Acropolis dedicated to the goddess Athena, the east and west pediments (see below) were decorated with relief figures representing two incidents in Athena's "life story." In addition, sculpture helped define the parts of a building, and these parts influenced the composition of the sculpture. Thus, figures had to be smaller or reclining to fit into the corners of the wide-based triangle or pediment, the top part of the wall of each short end of a columned temple (page 48). Artistic solutions to such technical problems varied in different periods. Other functional parts of buildings were vividly decorated, too (page 34).

Almost all Greek architecture and sculpture was brilliantly colored originally. The stone reliefs and round statues were painted in strong red, blue, yellow, enlivened with gold leaf. Terracotta (baked clay) sculpture was usually painted before firing. Even bronzes were polished and shining, and varied with eyes, lashes and lips inlaid with other materials. The plain white statues and ruined buildings, the greenish bronze surfaces that we know were not at all to Greek tastes.

At about 480 B.C., the Classical period began and lasted until the end of the fifth century. Just before this time, the Greeks had been warring with the Persians who already controlled East Greece (in Asia Minor). In celebration of the defeat of the Persian attack on the Greek mainland, an ambitious building program was initiated that was to last several decades. The most imposing result of this activity that demanded the financial and spiritual support of the whole population was the Parthenon on the Acropolis in Athens and its colossal statue of the patron goddess, Athena. Other richly decorated temples were raised in sacred sanctuaries such as Olympia (page 54), and some of the few sculptors who gained individual recognition in their own time were active, Myron (page 66) and Polykleitos (pages 56 and 58) among them.

The Peloponnesian Wars (431–404 B.C.) and the defeat of Athens, the leading Greek city-state, by Sparta were years of privation and stress for all Greeks. It is significant that, during the long years of the wars which drained economic resources, artistic activity diminished very little, and that some of Greece's most powerful playwrights (Sophocles, Euripides and Aristophanes) produced their mature works, and philosophy and history were pursued with vigor by Socrates, Thucydides and others.

The fourth century, until 323 B.C., is sometimes called the Late Classical period. Whatever it is called, philosophers and orators like Plato, Demosthenes and Aristotle were creative at this time, as the power of the city-states dwindled and finally came to an end with the conquest of Greek lands by the Macedonians and the rise to power of Alexander the Great, who was to extend the Greek world as far as India. Among the few artists of this time whose names we know, Praxiteles (pages 80, 82 and 84) and Lysippos (page 86) stand out. The latter established a new canon for representing the human body and, most important, went further toward expanding from the single, frontal view and restricted inner motion of most earlier statues (page 28) to movement into the spectator's space (page 86). Lysippos, as official sculptor of Alexander, was famous for his many portraits of the great leader.

Chance preservation has left us a larger proportion of original sculpture of the Hellenistic period than of earlier centuries; for the Classical period, we must deal of necessity with copies which may be far from reflecting the real spirit and artistic intent of the sculptor. Relief sculpture in Hellenistic times achieves an extraordinary amount of expressiveness by using endless variety of pose, lively and lifelike carving of all parts of the body, and dramatic use of flowing and flapping drapery; the relief decoration of the Great Altar of Zeus at Pergamon (Asia Minor) exemplifies all this to perfection.

Another outstanding feature of Hellenistic sculpture was the portrait. While the idea of representing particular persons as they really looked was not new to this epoch, portraiture reached a very high level of individuality during the third and second centuries. In the fifth and fourth centuries, a portrait usually emphasized the idealized character or the symbols of the subject's profession or social role (pages 42 and 76). Hellenistic artists, however, stressed expression of emotional and physical states not only in representations of famous persons (page 92) and mythological figures but of ordinary, anonymous people, too (page 110). The ideal in physical beauty and the fascination of using drapery in almost super-realistic effects continued (pages 107 and 100).

The year 146 B.C. saw the plundering of Corinth by the Romans. Sixty years later, Athens was laid waste by the new rulers of the Mediterranean, and Greece became part of the Roman Empire. Greek artists and craftsmen were still highly respected and continued to work for Roman patrons throughout the Empire in the tradition of their ancestors into the second century A.D. The echoes of Greek art were heard and reinterpreted in the Renaissance (fifteenth and sixteenth centuries A.D.) and still later in Neoclassic art of the late eighteenth and nineteenth centuries.

Jean L. Keith,
The Brooklyn Museum

Contents

FOURTH CENTURY (400–323 B.C.)

HELLENISTIC PERIOD (323-50 B.C.)

Preface

This book is not intended to be a history of Greek art or a treatise on Greek sculpture but simply to be a pictorial study, with brief explanatory text, of the amazing and unparalleled development of Greek sculpture through the centuries. It is hoped that the drawings will trace the transition from primitive carving and modeling to sculpture that is acclaimed as the greatest the world has ever seen.

From the time I first drew plaster replicas of Greek sculpture as an art student, long ago, I have had a great interest in sculpture. Although my training was in the field of drawing and painting rather than sculpture, my feeling for the third-dimensional quality of sculpture has, I believe, been a strong and constant influence on my work.

Although I have specialized for thirty years in drawing of horses as my work, I have always kept my feeling and interest in sculpture, and particularly Greek sculpture, and have sketched from these figures whenever possible. A European trip in 1965 gave me an opportunity to draw in the Louvre for several months. Since that museum has one of the finest collections of Greek art,

I made many drawings of these statues, just for study and pleasure.

My editor, interested in seeing what I had done abroad, saw the drawings and suggested a book on the subject. The idea appealed to me greatly and plans for the following year were made to get further material for this project.

As most European museums are not heated, sunny Sicily seemed a good starting point for the winter months. There were many Greek colonies on this island as early as 600 B.C., as attested to by the great temples in Agrigento, Selinunte and Segesta which compare favorably with the finest in Greece. Obviously, among the colonists, there were skilled and highly trained craftsmen. Marble was not found in Sicily but the carvers found the native limestone a satisfactory substitute as can be seen from the sculptures in the Sicilian museums. Syracuse was once one of the greatest and richest of Greek cities. Probably many of its fine examples of sculpture from Greece were imported. The beautiful Landolina Venus in the National Museum, Syracuse, is of marble. Furthermore, the workmanship and artistry is such that it may have come from the Greek mainland. However, in the museums of Gela, Agrigento and Palermo there are many carvings in limestone and figures in terracotta that are obviously of local origin. Even in these early efforts the instinct for fine design and simple form is as pronounced as that found in Athens itself. Ornament and decoration were always present, restrained and effective.

Greece has been despoiled of so much of its sculpture that less is to be found there than one might think. The Elgin Marbles from the Parthenon frieze were taken to England—"stolen," so Byron insisted. Much earlier the Roman conquerors carried all they could to Rome.

The Naples National Museum is especially rich in Greek sculpture, and the building is so spacious that I could see all to perfection. The director was particularly gracious and cooperative. Seeing that I was working under great difficulty because the vantage point I needed to draw the Doryphoros was in line with the path of the crowds of visitors, he permitted me to work on Sunday, a day when the museum was closed.

It is interesting to note the difference in quality of work that can come from the hand of the copyist. The Doryphoros is considered a fine and true copy and it surely must be, for it is a magnificent work of art. The heroic Herakles in the next gallery, despite its impressive power, has not been so fortunate in finding a copyist. The modeling—particularly in legs and calves—is overdone to create tension. You have only to compare it with the athlete scraping himself with a strigil, in the Vatican, to realize that the original bronze by Lysippos must have been quite different from the copy.

Although the Vatican Museum is rich in Greek sculpture, its limited space often makes for crowding. Since this museum attracts larger crowds than any other that comes to mind, except perhaps the Louvre, it was very difficult to work there. There was a still further problem that presented itself when I tried to draw the famous *Belvedere Torso* of Apollonius that Michelangelo so admired. It is mounted on a turntable. The viewer can turn the handle and see the statue from all sides. This seemed a novelty that no visitor could resist and soon I was ready to give up on my drawings. A museum guard noticed my problem and came over and stood in front of the handle so that the sculpture would be stationary for my drawing. This sort of courtesy and consideration was often given and much appreciated.

I recall one such instance that I feel was the greatest compliment I ever received. An attendant at the Athens Museum looked at me with a slightly jaundiced eye when I set up my folding sketch-stool and opened my portfolio. Some time later he came over to view my drawing. He then went and brought me his own chair which he insisted on my using for my drawing materials.

These are not casual sketches. Each drawing is the result of many hours—often days—of work. Every effort was made to be as accurate as possible in representing the sculpture. If there is any accentuation of lines and forms that create the rhythm and movement of design, this is not intentional. However, it is possible that an artist will unconsciously stress that which he most admires. The purpose at all times was to try to show the qualities that make these statues masterpieces.

To that end, such discoloration as time has made to the surface that could confuse the modeling has been omitted, as have all physical details of backgrounds. It is hoped that this will give a clearer impression of this sculpture—the greatest that we have.

—C.W.A.

This figure of a horse, in pose and general proportions, is otherwise so accurate that it is hard to determine whether the inordinately small body was done intentionally for decorative reasons. At any rate this small bronze gives a stronger sense of a proud horse than many realistic efforts of a later time.

HORSE
Bronze; height 6 5/16"
Mid-eighth century B.C.
Found on the Peloponnesos, possibly Olympia
Berlin, State Museum

This small bronze figure looks much like the primitive sculpture of Africa, but three centuries will show a development without parallel in the history of art.

WARRIOR
Bronze; height 8 1/16"
End of eighth century B.C.
Found on the Acropolis, Athens
Athens, National Museum

Probably the sculptor had never seen a lion—nevertheless he created a powerful and interesting animal with a look of intense ferocity. Again we see the fine design that is never missing, even in the earliest and most primitive of Greek art.

LION
Limestone; width at paws about 16"
Late seventh century B.C.
Found on the island of Corfu in 1843
Corfu, Museum   25

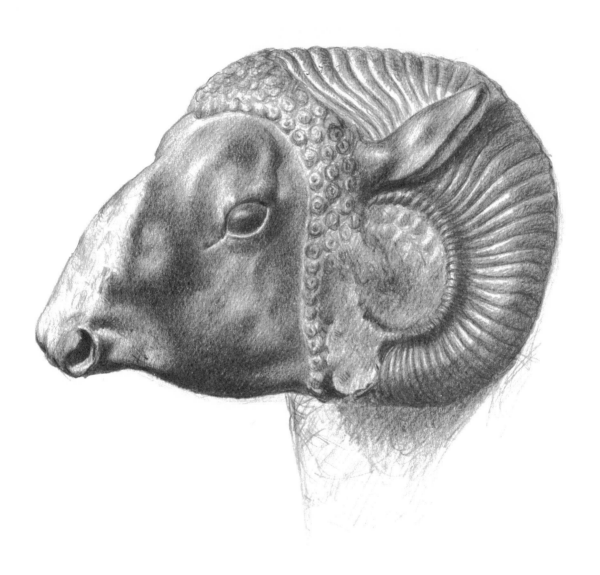

As Greek sculptors became more skilled in realistic representation they retained their instinctive feeling for proportion and decoration that marked their work as far back as the ninth century B.C. Locks or strands of hair were represented not by an indiscriminate mass of lines but by cunningly contrived shapes that added immensely to the decorative quality, yet blended perfectly with the realism of observation.

HEAD OF A RAM
Marble
Sixth century B.C.
From Eleusis
Sparta, Museum

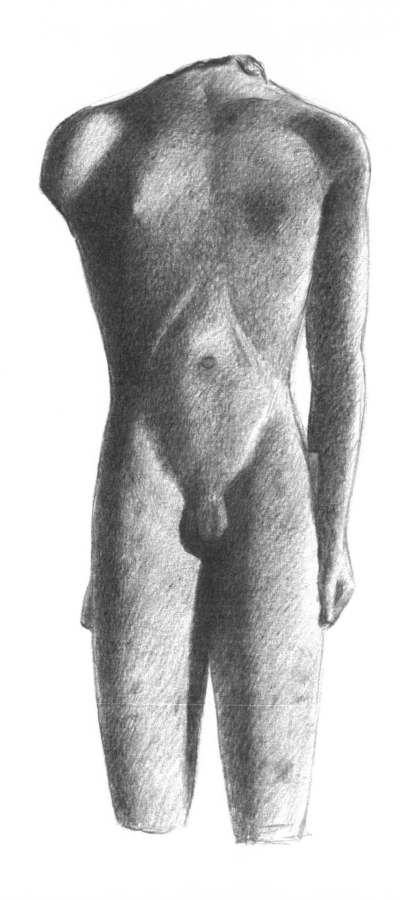

The first of the so-called *kouroi*, figures depicting young athletes, had a definite Egyptian feeling in its simplified form and stiff posture. The Greeks, however, were not satisfied with such a formal representation. Soon a more lifelike quality began to be shown; modeling of the breasts, muscles shown in the loins and a definite feeling of structure of the pelvis. The legs were no longer cylinders but were modeled with kneecap and defined muscles in the thigh and calf. All of this was not quite correct, for knowledge of anatomy was still not complete, but it was a long step forward toward an obvious goal.

KOUROS
Marble; height 3' 10 7/8"
Mid-sixth century B.C.
Found near Megara Hyblaia in 1940
Syracuse, National Museum 29

This head is a development of the *kouros* head. It has the same smile and formal features without individuality. The modeling is more subtle and realistic and the hair has more decorative quality. It is definitely a step forward toward lifelike representation.

HEAD OF A RIDER, the "RAMPIN HEAD"
Marble; height 11 3/8"
Mid-sixth century B.C.
From the Rampin Collection
Paris, Louvre   31

It is clearly shown in this late *kouros* that Greek sculptors were not content with a formalized, decorative representation of the human figure but were striving for a realistic representation. Compared to the earlier one we have seen (page 28), where anatomical forms were only vaguely suggested, this figure is almost lifelike, but still the stiffness of form persists and only the advance of one foot indicates the movement of walking.

Not until Polykleitos showed the way in the fifth century B.C. did Greek sculptors fully realize how important a part the entire body plays in a walking pose—how one shoulder drops and the angle of the pelvis changes as each leg carries the weight. Nonetheless this figure shows a decided advance in observation of surface characteristics.

KOUROS, MEMORIAL OF KRIOSOS
Marble; height 6' 4 3/8"
Late sixth century B.C.
Found at Anavyssos in 1936 and 1938
Athens, National Museum   33

These waterspouts from Euryalis, Sicily, are quite realistic. The artist obviously had a real knowledge of his subject and had the skill to portray it. Note the excellent sense of design in the handling of the mane and forms of the head.

LION WATERSPOUTS
Marble; height 9 7/8"
Fifth century B.C.
Probably from Euryalis, Sicily
Syracuse, National Museum   35

Pheidias—"most famous of all who wrought the images of the gods"—is said to have begun as a painter and to have become a sculptor fairly late in life. His progress as a sculptor was great and striking. He was chosen to make a giant statue of Athena—a wooden core overlaid with thin pieces of gold and ivory—and was placed in charge of all the sculpture in the Parthenon.

Athena was evidently a favorite subject of Pheidias. The Athena shown here must be a fine copy; it has the dignity and purity of line characteristic of his work. (The greatness of Pheidias shines through copies; we have no single verifiable work by his hands.) In Pheidias' figures, none of them nudes, the body shows through subtly and beautifully. His handling of the folds of the *chiton,* or tunic—which could easily have become monotonous—is the very essence of perfect design.

The works of the great Pheidias were never mere showpieces of sculptural virtuosity. The feeling is that they were accomplished primarily for those who were portrayed—the gods.

ATHENA
Marble
Fifth century B.C.
Paris, Louvre   37

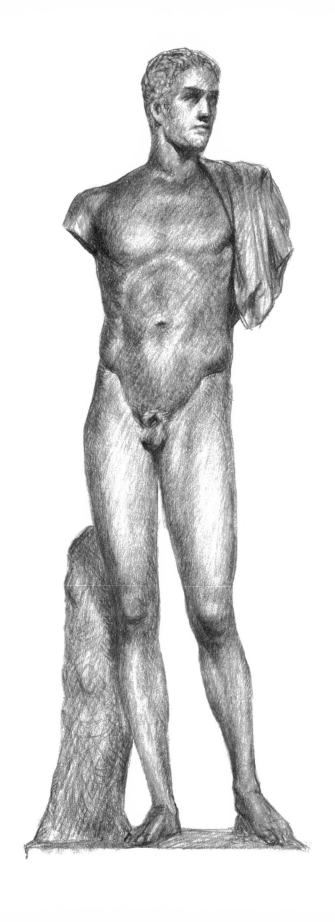

The first of the great sculptors of the Classical period to concentrate his efforts on truly individual likeness in his work seems to have been Kresilas. The figures of the gods were, of course, idealized types, and this must have been true also of those statues made in honor of victors in the Olympic games, for they were all handsome, with regular features and magnificent bodies, but differing very little in appearance.

Kresilas did nude figures superbly. The same feeling for a broad deep torso that characterized Polykleitos' work is shown here, but his figures are taller and not quite so compact as Polykleitos' *Doryphoros* (page 56). One of Kresilas' most famous works was his *Diomedes*. The original in bronze has disappeared but a number of copies exist. The one in the Louvre, shown here, has the power and grace that characterized all his work. It must have been famous in its day, for many copies have been found.

DIOMEDES
Original by Kresilas*
Marble
Fifth century B.C.
Paris, Louvre 39

---

* "Original" here and following indicates that the sculpture illustrated is a copy, whereas medium, date and location refer to illustrated work.

This carving in low relief was done by an unknown local sculptor in a small Greek city. An artist of any era might be proud of its skilled execution and design. The relief is so flat that less than an inch separates its highest surface from its lowest, yet it is full and varied and has much strength and volume.

GRAVE STELE WITH RIDER ON HORSEBACK
Limestone; height 3' 11 1/4"
Fifth century B.C.
Found near Thespis in 1814
Athens, National Museum   41

It was Leonidas, king of Sparta, who, with a small band of heroic warriors, held the pass at Thermopylae against the Persian army of Xerxes and gave their lives to delay the enemy until the Greeks could rally their full strength. And it was he who, when told that the Persian force was so great that their arrows in flight would cover the sun, is said to have replied, "So much the better. We shall fight in the shade."

Though the face of this statue has suffered from time and the eyes are gone from the sockets, there is still the look of an indomitable man: a hero. The great power of the torso reinforces this feeling.

LEONIDAS
Marble; height 2′ 7″
Fifth century B.C.
From Sparta
Athens, National Museum 43

This horse's head in terracotta was probably done by a native sculptor in Sicily, for Greeks on the mainland worked primarily in bronze and marble. Since the work was done at the same time as the frieze of the Parthenon, we can compare it with the horses there, and it does not suffer in the comparison.

HEAD OF HORSE
Terracotta; height 11"
Fifth century B.C.
Gela, Museum   45

These two figures, representing the Athenians Harmodios and Aristogeiton, were so called because the men they portray gave their lives to rid Athens of two tyrants that ruled the city— Hipparchos and Hippias. They succeeded in killing Hipparchos but were themselves killed in the ensuing fight before they could deal with Hippias.

A few years later Hippias was driven into exile, and bronze statues by the sculptors, Kritios and Nesiotes, were erected in honor of the two patriots. These have since disappeared and this is a Roman copy of the originals.

The originals were done in 477 B.C., before the great period ushered in by Pheidias, Polykleitos, and Kresilas, but already true proportions and vigorous action are strongly evident.

THE TYRANNICIDES, HARMODIOS AND ARISTOGEITON
Original
Marble; height about 6 1/2'
Early fifth century B.C.
Found in Tivoli
Naples, National Museum   47

Since all the sculpture of the Parthenon was done under Pheidias' supervision, he probably made the preliminary studies for much of it. It seems unlikely that such a sculptor could refrain from picking up mallet and chisel for finishing touches here and there or that some part might not interest him enough to do it with his own hands. This horse's head is so notable in the pediment that it might well be by Pheidias himself.

HEAD OF HORSE
Marble; length 2' 8"
Mid-fifth century B.C.
From the East Pediment of the Parthenon, Acropolis, Athens
London, British Museum   49

As we know, the Romans had the greatest admiration for Greek sculpture, and they had sent back to Rome everything that could be transported. But ships were small and storms violent, and it is perhaps due to this fact that we have this original Greek bronze of the great Classical period—a true masterpiece. This heroic-sized statue was found in the sea off Cape Artemision on the north coast of the island Euboea.

In this powerful statue the modeling of the figure, with such a great feeling of movement, is superb. The movement is not exaggerated though. The muscles move and flow, each does its part. We cannot identify the sculptor—I would think of Myron, yet authorities do not feel there is evidence of this in the style of modeling.

POSEIDON or ZEUS
Bronze; 6' 10"
Mid-fifth century B.C.
Found in the sea off Cape Artemision, Euboea, in 1926 and 1928
Athens, National Museum 51

The fact that the statue is over life-size makes it certain that it represents a god, for athletes were usually represented life-size. The power and grandeur in the bearded head is also godlike, so the subject is identified as Poseidon hurling a trident, or Zeus a thunderbolt. Possibly, if representing Poseidon, the statue was done to commemorate the shipwreck of the Persian fleet off Cape Artemision, for to the maritime Greeks, so dependent on their ships in war, Poseidon was a protective god.

Detail of POSEIDON or ZEUS

This was one of the metopes of the temple of Zeus at Olympia and, judging from the life and movement as well as the skillful modeling, one of the finest. The torso of Herakles is a magnificent accomplishment with a power and movement not often seen in sculpture. This Herakles is not as massive in musculature as some that were carved but he looks like a tremendously powerful man who could rise to any occasion.

HERAKLES AND THE CRETAN BULL
Marble; height about 5' 2"
Mid-fifth century B.C.
Metope from the Temple of Zeus at Olympia
Paris, Louvre   55

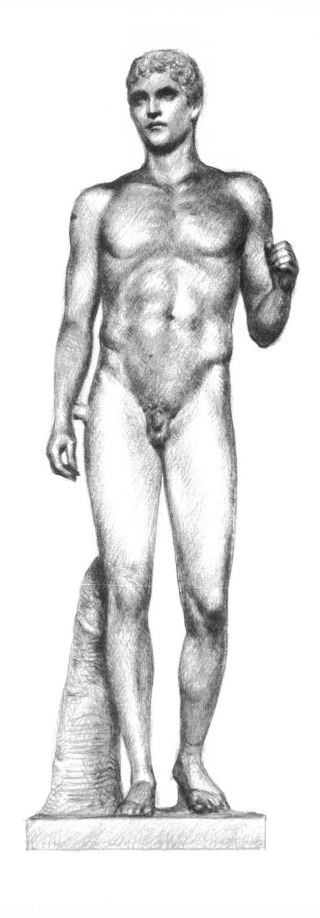

In the later part of the Archaic period the attempt had been made to give a feeling of movement to the *kouroi* (statues of standing youths). The first of the Archaic figures had their feet firmly planted together on the plinths; then one foot was put forward in an attempt to give the appearance of a man walking. Since the movement was entirely in the legs, the figures were stiff and motionless. Knowledge of anatomy at that time was slight and superficial, but this was soon to be remedied by Polykleitos, who could give more life and movement to a walking figure than others accomplished with the most extreme and violent poses.

Polykleitos' fame rests mostly on this famous statue—the *Doryphoros*. The best known copy of it is in the National Museum of Naples, from which the drawing was made. This figure represents Polykleitos' ideal proportions for the male figure. The broad, powerful shoulders, the square, deep chest, and the rhythm and balance throughout so satisfied the sculptors of the day that the statue was called the "Canon," meaning the ideal of proportions in the human body. The style of the torso of the *Doryphoros,* wide and deep in the chest and powerful throughout the loins, is typical of all Polykleitos' work.

Perhaps there is nothing in Greek art comparable to the power and rhythm that Polykleitos attained in the male torso. Here, in the *Doryphoros,* apparently for the first time, was seen a walking figure in which the pelvis showed the shift of weight of the body with all muscles moving in coordination, and portrayed such perfection that the Greek world marveled. It is no less miraculous today.

SPEAR CARRIER, the "DORYPHOROS"
Original by Polykleitos
Marble; height 6' 6"
Mid-fifth century B.C.
Naples, National Museum   57

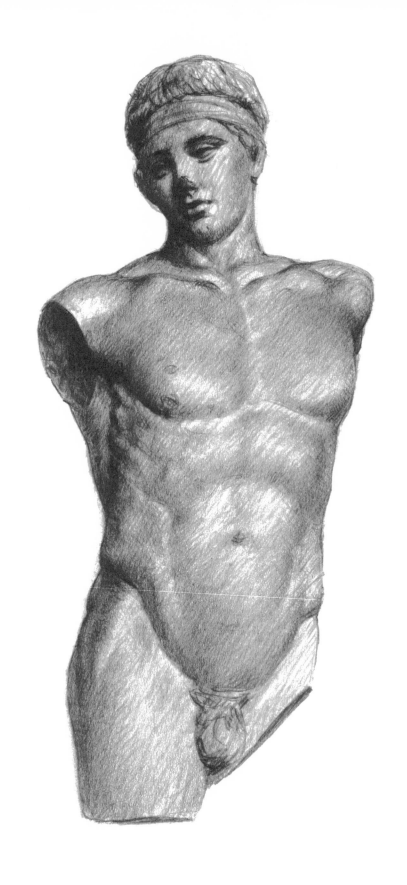

Another work by Polykleitos of almost equal fame is this *Dia-doumenos*. The original no longer exists but there are many copies and fragments of copies, as indeed there are of much of the artist's work. The Louvre copy is shown here, and again we see the power and rhythm of muscles that characterize Poly-kleitos' work. He wished to portray an athlete at the very height of physical condition, and no one surpassed him in this field.

YOUTH TYING A FILLET AROUND HIS HEAD,
   the "DIADOUMENOS"
Original by Polykleitos
Marble
Late fifth century B.C.
Paris, Louvre   59

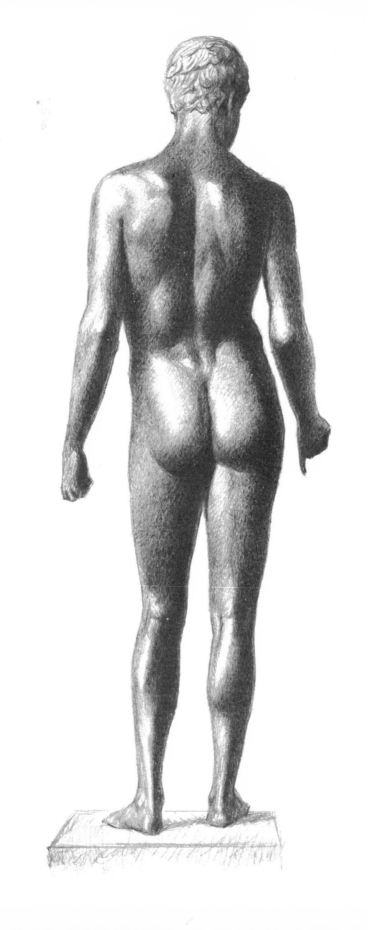

This bronze is attributed to Polykleitos, or his school, and the fine, solid modeling throughout makes this seem a logical conclusion. No other sculptor comes to mind who handled masculine form with the same solidity and simplicity. If it is not by Polykleitos himself, it could well be by one of his most talented students.

YOUTH BEARING A GIFT
School of Polykleitos (?)
Bronze; height 8 1/4"
Late fifth century B.C.
Paris, Louvre   61

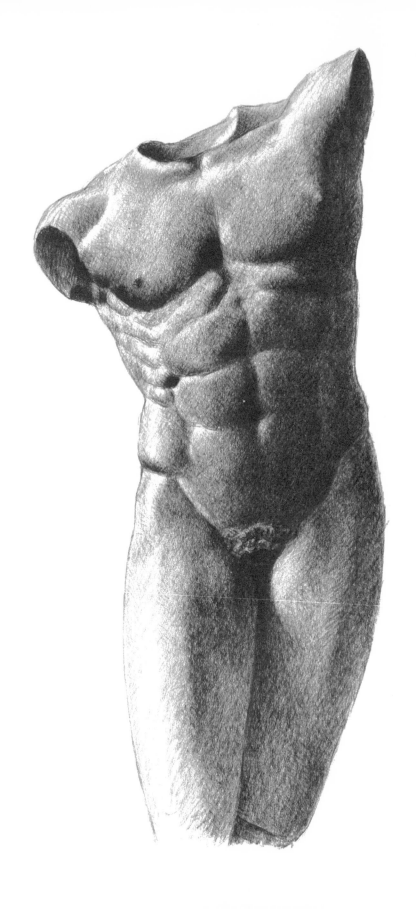

This headless torso has much of the wonderful form and move-ment that Polykleitos achieved in his *Diadoumenos* (page 58). It is credited to a sculptor named Pythagoras, but from its quality alone it could well belong to any of the great sculptors that were well known.

MALE TORSO
Original perhaps by Pythagoras
Marble
Mid-fifth century B.C.
Paris, Louvre 63

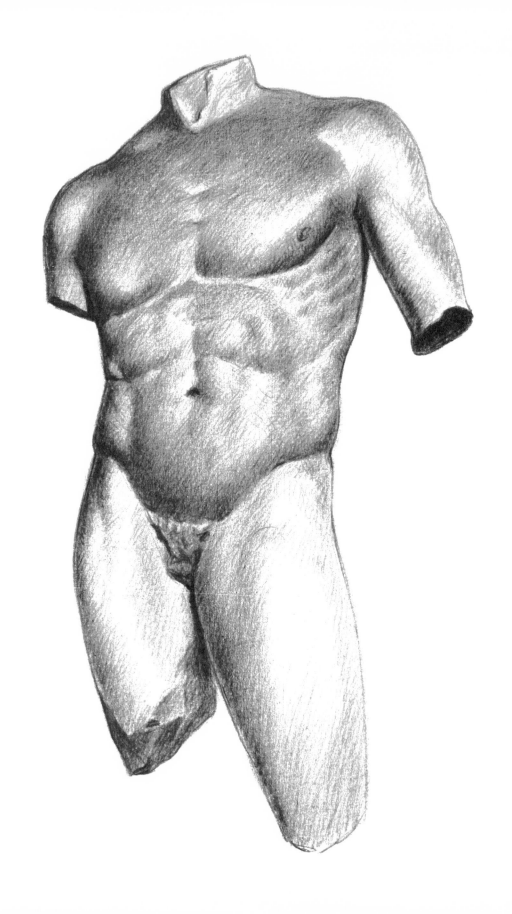

This torso is beautifully and sensitively modeled with much of the breadth of shoulder and depth of chest associated with the work of Polykleitos. The carver was obviously a true master of the human figure.

MALE TORSO
Original, School of Polykleitos
Marble; height 3' 11 1/4''
Late fifth century B.C.
Boston, Museum of Fine Arts

Of Myron, slightly older than Pheidias or Polykleitos, we know little; only two works have been attributed to him with certainty. His famous *Diskobolos,* however, speaks eloquently for itself. Sculpted in a time when the representation of a figure just walking was an innovation, its vivid and extreme movement of a discus thrower is a magnificent example of rhythmic action.

Some have criticized the *Diskobolos* for anatomical shortcomings, but what Myron attempted here was of utmost difficulty, for even an expert athlete could hold this pose only briefly, and the slightest variation in the model's pose would produce a different arrangement of the anatomy. It is also possible that the copyists of the bronze original, even if they were conscientious, may have lacked the knowledge of how muscles produce forms in a figure, and how they moved. Lacking such knowledge, they could only copy the undulations of the form before them. The difference in the seeing might be slight, but it would be there.

DISCUS THROWER, the "DISKOBOLOS"
Original by Myron
Marble; lifesize
Mid-fifth century B.C.
Rome, National Museum   67

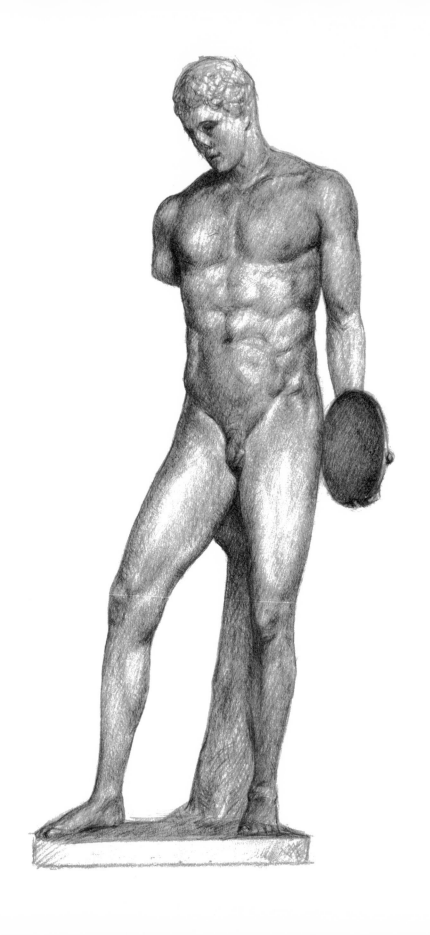

Naukydes portrayed this discus thrower standing poised, ready to begin the throw. We saw the discus thrower in full movement in Myron's *Diskobolos* (page 66). Such is the modeling in this lithe and powerful body that even in repose it suggests almost as much action as the *Diskobolos*. An artist capable of creating this figure must have produced many a masterpiece.

DISCUS THROWER
Original by Naukydes (?)
Marble: height 5′ 6 1/2″
End fifth century B.C.
Found on the Via Appia Antica, near Rome
Paris, Louvre

Kallimachos is a sculptor of whom little is known, but this *Aphrodite,* with the form so beautifully modeled through the filmy drapery, speaks of a consummate artist, and is attributed to him.

APHRODITE, "VENUS GENITRIX"
Original perhaps by Kallimachos
Marble; height 5′ 3 3/4″
Late fifth century B.C.
Paris, Louvre

This figure, in relief, was part of the balustrade around the Temple of Athena Nike on the Acropolis. Of the many lovely figures of the group, this is perhaps the finest of all. Never has drapery been handled with more consummate artistry in rhythm and design. The diagram below shows that even in bare outline the movement and rhythm are magnificent.

NIKE LACING HER SANDAL
Marble; height 3′ 6″
End fifth century B.C.
From the balustrade around
Temple of Athena Nike, Athenian Acropolis
Athens, Acropolis Museum   73

Again we have a bronze figure that might well be by the great master, Polykleitos. The balance and handling of form shows the sure mastery of movement in repose that marked all his work. Since it is much smaller than life, and the classic masters usually worked in life-size or larger, it could be a copy of one of his works.

STANDING GIRL
School of Polykleitos (?)
Bronze; height 9 7/8"
Late fifth or early fourth century B.C.
Found at Beroea in Macedonia
Munich, Museum (of Ancient Minor Arts) antiker Kleinkunst   75

Homer, a legendary figure to us, was almost as much a legend to the Greeks of the great Classical period, for he lived many centuries before. He was to the Greeks the greatest of their poets: what Shakespeare is to us—and perhaps even more.

This head was the sculptor's conception of the great blind poet. As we look at it, we find it hard to believe the portrait was not done from life.

The sculptor is not known, but in this head portraiture reached a very high standard. Rather than a formal, idealized type, this is an intensely individualized rendering—not a man but *the* man. The very look of a vision far beyond that of most men shows in the blind eyes beneath the deep brows.

HOMER
Marble; height 13″
Fourth century B.C.
Naples, National Museum

This truly magnificent Athena, simple and dignified, shows a subtlety of modeling seen only in the works of great masters. The handling of the drapery with its beauty and variety of design and the sense of the figure beneath would be worthy of Pheidias himself.

ATHENA
Marble; height 4' 7 1/8''
Fourth century B.C.
Found in Crete
Paris, Louvre

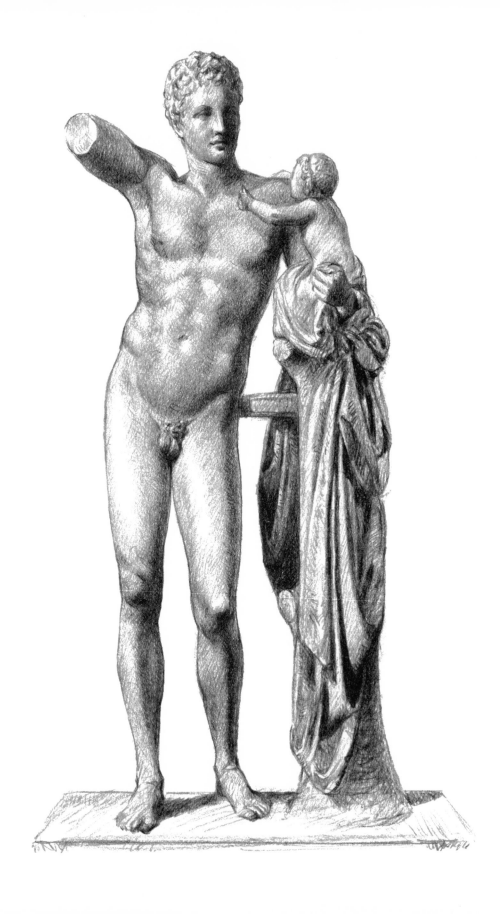

With the passing of those giants—Pheidias, Polykleitos, Myron, and Kresilas—Greek sculpture entered a period where the work of all the many artists who modeled and carved was capable and craftsmanlike but not outstanding. Then in the middle of the fourth century appeared a sculptor who was second only to Pheidias in fame and was perhaps even more admired in his day. This was Praxiteles.

Praxiteles was possibly the son, or perhaps the brother, of Kephisodotos, himself a sculptor of great ability. Kephisodotos' Athena in the Louvre has much of the feeling of simplicity found in the work of Pheidias, although Kephisodotos shows a grace and ease in his figures that make them more human than austere and godlike. Praxiteles carried this human quality even further. His figures were relaxed, sometimes almost languid, in their grace.

Up to this time the leading sculptors had worked primarily in bronze—marble was for the copyist. However, Praxiteles developed such skill in the use of marble that it became as much admired as bronze as a material, possibly even more so. There is one work in marble that has survived and is thought to be from Praxiteles' own hand. The famous *Hermes and the Infant Dionysos,* found where the statue was known to have stood, is of such masterly workmanship in modeling and finish that most authorities think it is an original.

HERMES AND THE INFANT DIONYSOS
Praxiteles
Marble; height 7'
Late fourth century B.C.
Found in Olympia in 1877
Olympia, Museum   81

It was as a sculptor of the female form that Praxiteles excelled all others in grace and beauty. Just as Polykleitos was able to put all that was strong and masculine into his figures, so Praxiteles incorporated the very essence of feminine grace and charm into his figures of women.

"APHRODITE OF ARLES"
Original by Praxiteles
Marble; height 6' 8 3/8"
Mid-fourth century B.C.
Paris, Louvre

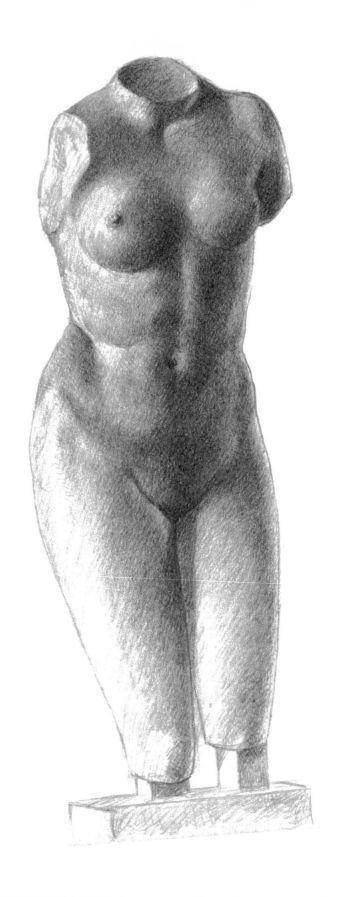

In pose, grace, and surface finish, this lovely torso strongly suggests Praxiteles' hand. It seems worthy of him for it has a loveliness seldom seen in sculpture of the adolescent feminine figure.

"APHRODITE OF CNIDUS"
Original by Praxiteles
Marble; height 3' 11 5/8"
Mid-fourth century B.C.
Paris, Louvre

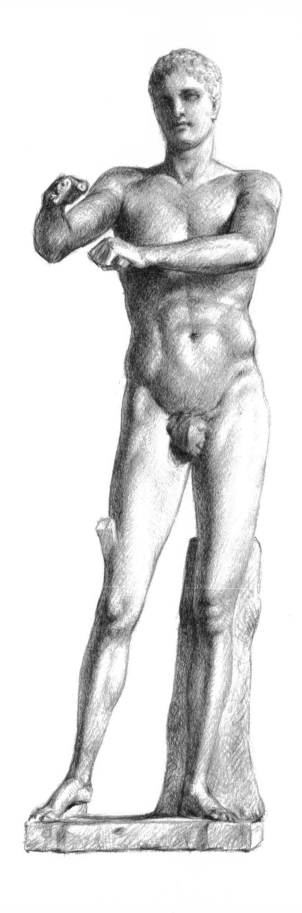

Lysippos was highly regarded in his day, and judging from the mention of many of his works by historians, he must have been a prolific artist, but little has survived, even in copies. This standing athlete, scraping himself with a strigil, is a taller and lither figure than the Polykleitan type but has the same feeling of movement throughout and shows marvelous anatomical modeling.

SCRAPER, the "APOXYOMENOS"
Original by Lysippos
Marble; height 6' 9"
Late fourth century B.C.
Rome, Vatican Museum   87

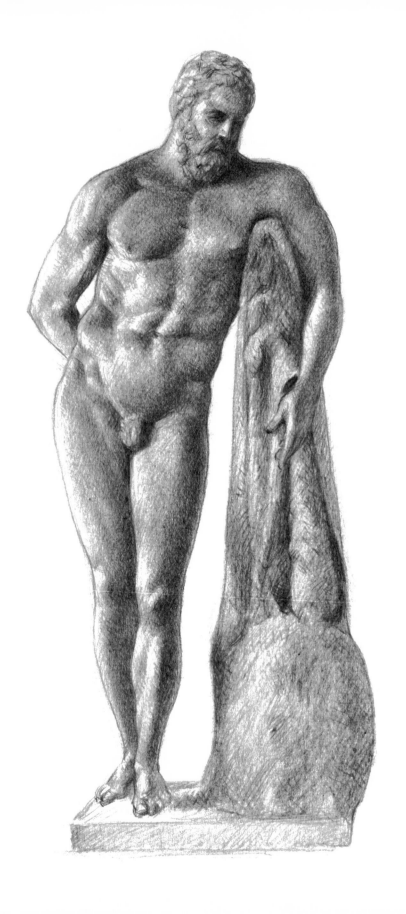

Herakles, strongest of heroes, was a favorite subject with ancient sculptors and painters. There are many conceptions of him to be found. All are, of course, powerful, but this heroic marble, more than ten feet high, seems most like the hero who could kill a lion with his bare hands.

He is shown resting from his Labors with his great muscles relaxed, and the three golden apples of Hesperides all but lost in his huge right hand.

Historians mention a bronze of this description that was done by Lysippos and this is supposed to be a copy of that work. It is signed with the name of Glykon, a copyist who worked in Roman Imperial times. Critics feel that he took liberties to make the work more in keeping with the taste of his day. Still, much of the feeling of power and movement characteristic of the great fourth-century sculptor remains.

"FARNESE HERAKLES"
Original by Lysippos, copy by Glykon
Marble; height about 9' 2"
Late fourth century B.C.
Found in the Baths of Caracalla, Rome, in 1540
Naples, National Museum

This lovely, sensitive head is a departure from the Classical treatment of form in Greek sculpture. In art as in poetry and drama the Greeks generally strove for the utmost clarity and conciseness of statement. But here the forms are very subtle, with softly turned edges that create a mysterious unique beauty.

That Rodin saw this sculpture and admired it is clear. That it influenced his handling of marble he readily admitted.

HEAD OF GIRL
Marble; height 1' 2 1/4"
End fourth century B.C.
Found on island of Chios during Crimean War, 1854–1856
Boston, Museum of Fine Arts 91

This is considered a portrait of a philosopher and it seems a logical assumption. It is definitely a portrait, for it has great individuality. Although the head is realistically treated the hair is a study in fine design. At first it might seem a disorderly mass of locks, but studied carefully, there is a rhythm and movement to the arrangement of the locks that are a pleasure to observe.

PHILOSOPHER
Bronze; height 11 3/8″
Second half of third century B.C.
Found in the sea off Antikythera in 1900–1901
Athens, National Museum   93

Perhaps nothing in Greek sculpture more completely follows the Greek maxim "Nothing in excess" than this broken or damaged figure. The action is so tense and dramatic that it would be easy for the artist to exaggerate and overmodel the muscles to increase the effect. The pose is so active that even a trained athlete could hold it only for a very short time, yet the anatomy here is so accurate and subtle that it must have been done from life.

The sculptor is uncertain. The Fallen Warrior may be a Gaulish warrior, based on nothing more than the fact that the length of limb indicates a tall figure, and the Gauls were men of great stature.

FALLEN WARRIOR
Marble; height 3' 1 3/8"
Second century B.C.
Found on Delos in 1883
Athens, National Museum   95

Most of the Greek sculpture found on the sites of the Greek settlements in Sicily are of limestone, for marble is not native to Sicily. Since this lovely statue is of marble and the modeling is that of a fine, well-trained sculptor, it was possibly brought over from Greece. Syracuse was one of the greatest and richest of Greek colonial cities so its leading citizens could well afford the finest art available.

APHRODITE, the "LANDOLINA VENUS"
Marble; 5' 5"
Second century B.C.
Syracuse, National Museum

This figure, half life-size, was part of a fountain above the Syracuse Theatre. It is one of several of similar size and treatment. The rhythmic presentation of the drapery is similar to that of figures done in Greece at this period, and since it is of marble it perhaps was imported from Greece. There is a grace and flow to the design that mark it as the work of a very fine artist.

STANDING WOMAN IN A CHITON
Marble; 3' 5/8"
Second century B.C.
From fountain above Theatre, Syracuse
Syracuse, National Museum

Here we have one of the greatest of the ancient Greek statues, this one an original marble. We have no knowledge of the sculptor of this masterpiece, except that he was thought to be of the school of Rhodes. The *Nike* was found at Samothrace and stood overlooking the sea, the pedestal shaped to represent the prow of a ship. Written records of the time, about 200 B.C., tell us that it was erected to commemorate a naval victory over Antiochus III, king of Syria. The statue is on a heroic scale, well over life-size, and was placed on a high rock so it could be seen from afar by approaching ships. There is no signature of the sculptor.

The "Winged Victory," as it is commonly called, now stands at the top of the long stairway leading to the painting galleries at the Louvre, where it dominates the whole approach.

The loss of the head and arms detracts but little from the feeling of power and movement of this marvelous figure. The wind from the sea so presses against the thin *chiton* that the figure is shown as clearly as if in the nude, and the swirl of the garments creates a design of movement rarely equaled.

The drapery alone is a marvel, not only of design, but for its complete reality. It is not too difficult to do such drapery on an unrealistic, stylized figure where it can be made to fit the design, but here any false note would ruin the whole. The movement of the drapery had to be realistic throughout, yet simplified for the final effect.

The statue must have lain long buried, probably in red clay,

NIKE OF SAMOTHRACE, the "WINGED VICTORY"
Marble; height 8'
Early second century B.C.
Found on Samothrace in 1863
Paris, Louvre

Another view of NIKE OF SAMOTHRACE,
the "WINGED VICTORY"

Diagram of NIKE OF SAMOTHRACE,
the "WINGED VICTORY"

for the originally white marble is deeply colored, almost to a brick hue in parts, and all of a golden reddish tone.

The "Winged Victory" is so complete as it stands that it is doubtful if the missing arms, or even the head, could add to the magnificence of its effect. In many of the ancient works of art, wings affixed to a figure do not seem to be a part of the figure at all, but merely attached appendages as symbols for identification. Here they seem actually to grow from the body as do wings of a bird. It is also worthwhile to study the arrangement of the feathers on the inside of the wings—truly a masterpiece of intricate and varied design. In this statue there is no area that is dull, dead, or static.

The diagram of the "Winged Victory" is an attempt to show the layman how the artist conceived his design. In this instance his main desire was to bring a surge and lift to the figure as it faced the sea.

The dark lines indicate the lines and forms that create the forward and upward thrust. They recur again and again in different intensity of form and from slightly different angles, each giving added impetus to the action.

Lines or shapes of equal division—halves, thirds and quarters—tend to be static and stop movement and are to be avoided, while divisions that are unequal and varied create a feeling of movement. This is very clear and evident in folds of drapery in Praxiteles' Athena and in Pheidias' magnificent figure of the same goddess.

The lighter lines here show how one shape or line in a design always relates to another and creates an additional rhythm of movement that the eye unconsciously follows.

As you turn into the long corridor leading to the sculpture galleries at the Louvre, the Venus de Milo stands at the end, shining like a beacon for the wayfarer. No matter how common-place it has become to you through the many reproductions, you are never quite prepared for it. Its beauty and grandeur take your breath away. It glows—it is a living thing.

It was found in 1820 in a cave on the island of Melos, and represents Aphrodite. Fragments of the arms were also found there, and though not complete there were enough that fitted exactly to give an idea of the complete statue as it was. No attempt has been made to restore the arms, which is fortunate—they could only detract from the beauty of the torso. The disposition of the arms in a figure is always a problem for the sculptor—so much so that many a latter-day nude has been sculpted as if the arms had been broken off. This leaves the torso a complete entity, shown at its best.

The Venus de Milo was presented to the king of France as a masterpiece of Praxiteles, whose fame at that time was greatest of all the ancient Greek sculptors. When the statue was set up, however, a broken part of the plinth, or base, which fitted so perfectly that there could be no doubt that it was part of the statue, bore the name of a sculptor entirely unknown. This caused

the greatest consternation, and after a hurried consultation between the court officials and the museum directors that part of the plinth disappeared before the presentation to the king, and was never seen again. An artist named Debay was present when the statue was first set up and made a careful drawing of the plinth with the missing piece in place, giving the sculptor's name.

Perhaps nothing could give us a better idea of how numerous were the very fine sculptors of ancient Greece than to find that one of the greatest works of art of all time was created by an artist entirely unknown to us, who was not even mentioned in any history of the period.

Most authorities place the Venus around the middle of the second century B.C.—possibly as late as 125 B.C. Following Praxiteles' lead, sculptors of the late Hellenistic period worked mostly in marble. A statue was not always made of one block of stone, but of several pieces joined together with dowel pins and fitted so beautifully that the joint could not be seen. This was true of the Venus de Milo which is made of two pieces of marble joined at the line of the drapery at the waist. Dowel holes also show that the arms were of separate pieces of marble. This is often a distinguishing mark of an original Greek work, for the Roman copies were generally made of a single block of marble.

Although the marble was originally pure white, age and the long time that it was buried have given it a golden sheen that cannot be described.

APHRODITE, the "VENUS DE MILO"
Marble; 6' 8"
Late second century B.C.
Found on the island of Melos in 1820
Paris, Louvre   107

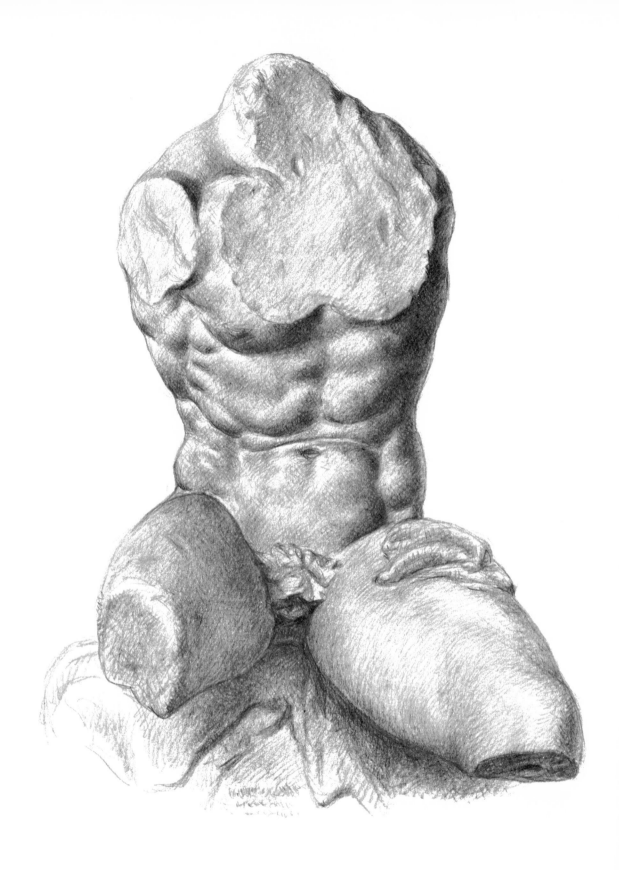

It was not usual for sculptors to sign their work until the Hellenistic period. We have two works signed by Apollonios that are enough to show that he was one of the best of Greek sculptors. The heroic torso in the Vatican Museum known as the *Belvedere Torso* has the power and movement we see in the work of Polykleitos. The head and neck are gone, the arms are broken off at the shoulder and the legs are broken above the knees, but it would be worth going to the museum merely to see this torso, if nothing else were there.

Michelangelo so admired the *Belvedere Torso* that he spoke of it as "my teacher." If you remember the vigor of the action in his sculpture, you can see that he was indeed influenced by this torso.

The power and development in this figure are on a heroic scale—it scarcely needs the lion skin upon which it is seated to identify it as representing Hercules.

It was found in Rome in the fifteenth century, buried under a cobbler's shop. The cobbler had used it for pounding leather, and the marks of this are still in evidence on the right thigh.

"BELVEDERE TORSO," perhaps Herakles
By Apollonios
Marble; height 5′ 2 5/8″
Early first century B.C.
Rome, Vatican Museum   109

This bronze figure of a seated boxer, nearly life-size, is a complete departure from the idealism Greek sculptors had shown in portraying the gods. This is brutal realism: obviously a true portrait of the man, with a powerfully developed body and small, rather bestial head, with cuts and welts—inflicted by leather thongs worn on the hands in this sport—clearly shown. It is also a departure in the treatment of the surface, which has more the character that Rodin used in his bronzes.

BOXER
By Apollonios
Bronze; height 4' 2 3/8"
Second to first century B.C.
Found in Rome in 1884
Rome, National Museum   111

For Further Reading

Bieber, Margarete. *The Sculpture of the Hellenistic Age*. Rev. ed. New York: Columbia University Press, 1961.

Boardman, John. *Greek Art*. New York: Praeger, 1964.

Lullies, Reinhard. *Greek Sculpture*. Rev. ed. New York: Abrams, 1957.

Richter, Gisela M. A. *A Handbook of Greek Art*. 5th ed. London: Phaidon, 1967.

Richter, Gisela M. A. *The Sculpture and Sculptors of the Greeks*. Rev. ed. New Haven, Connecticut: Yale University Press, 1950.